YOU CHOOSE

LIFE OR DEATH ON A MOUNTAIN

AN INTERACTIVE SURVIVAL ADVENTURE

BY MEGAN CLENDENAN

CAPSTONE PRESS
a capstone imprint

Published by Capstone Press, an imprint of Capstone
1710 Roe Crest Drive, North Mankato, Minnesota 56003
capstonepub.com

Copyright © 2025 by Capstone. All rights reserved. No part of this publication may be reproduced in whole or in part, or stored in a retrieval system, or transmitted in any form or by any means, electronic, mechanical, photocopying, recording, or otherwise, without written permission of the publisher.

Library of Congress Cataloging-in-Publication Data is available on the Library of Congress website.

ISBN: 9781669088486 (hardcover)
ISBN: 9781669088455 (paperback)
ISBN: 9781669088462 (ebook PDF)

Summary: Readers face the challenges of being lost on a mountain, inspired by the experiences of real people.

Editorial Credits
Editor: Mandy Robbins; Designer: Dina Her; Media Researcher: Jo Miller; Production Specialist: Tori Abraham

Image Credits:
AP Images: Nick Perry, 107; Getty Images: Alex Ratson, 8, Capelle.r, 77, Charlie Milliard, 15, David W. Thompson, 40, Grant Faint, 80, Jonathan Beckett, 6, july7th, 10, Paola Giannoni, 35; Shutterstock: ALEX_UGALEK, 71, ansharphoto, 72, christopher babcock, 4, Coppee Audrey, 89, critterbiz, 23, easy camera, 98, Galyna Andrushko, 20, Gustavo Frazao, 67, Jack Nevitt, 59, Kelly vanDellen, cover, 1, LuismiCSS, 102, Matushchak Anton, 86, Vaclav Sebek, 52, Victor Grecu, 62, vk_st, 101

Design Elements:
Shutterstock: EB Adventure Photograph, Here, oxinoxi

Any additional websites and resources referenced in this book are not maintained, authorized, or sponsored by Capstone. All product and company names are trademarks™ or registered® trademarks of their respective holders.

Printed and bound in the USA. 6121

TABLE OF CONTENTS

INTRODUCTION
ABOUT YOUR ADVENTURE 5

CHAPTER 1
LOST IN THE MOUNTAINS 7

CHAPTER 2
COAST MOUNTAIN SUMMIT 11

CHAPTER 3
CRATERS OF COSTA RICA 41

CHAPTER 4
ADVENTURE IN THE ALPS 73

CHAPTER 5
MOUNTAIN SURVIVAL 99

TRUE STORIES OF
MOUNTAIN SURVIVAL 106
S.T.O.P. TO SURVIVE 108
OTHER PATHS TO EXPLORE....... 109
GLOSSARY.................... 110
READ MORE 111
INTERNET SITES 111
ABOUT THE AUTHOR 112

INTRODUCTION

ABOUT YOUR ADVENTURE

YOU are exploring magnificent and wild mountains when you find yourself lost. With few resources and no help, what direction will you go? Threats are everywhere—hunger, thirst, dangerous terrain, bad weather, and mighty predators. It's a constant struggle just to live through another day. YOU CHOOSE what path to take. Will you make it back to safety or die trying?

Turn the page to begin your adventure.

CHAPTER 1

LOST IN THE MOUNTAINS

You descend a steep mountain trail through dense trees and green shrubs. You watch where you step as you navigate roots and rocks to avoid getting hurt. On the mountain, even a small injury like a sprained ankle could have big consequences.

Something doesn't feel quite right. Was this the trail you came up? There were trail markers, but you can't remember when you last saw one.

Turn the page.

On the way up, you heard a creek rushing. Now you don't. You study your surroundings. Nothing looks familiar. You pull out your phone, but there's no signal. You aren't sure where you are—or which direction you should go.

With a sinking feeling, you realize you are lost. How did this happen? You set out this morning for an adventure in the mountains, but somewhere along the way, you took a wrong turn. You gaze up, searching for a familiar landmark, but the peaks in the distance are shadowed by dusk. The sun is setting, and you are hungry. In the shadows, wildlife may lurk. You are on your own in a life-or-death situation.

You must stay calm. Still, you can't help thinking back and wondering how you wound up here.

- To have gone exploring the Pacific Northwest's Coast Mountains, turn to page 11.

- To have gotten lost on a field study in Costa Rica, turn to page 41.

- To be lost in the snowy Alps of France, turn to page 73.

CHAPTER 2

COAST MOUNTAIN SUMMIT

"We're going to climb that?" Lila peers out the window as you arrive at the trailhead. "Wow!"

"Yep!" you say.

You look up at the misty Coast Mountains, with their towering granite cliffs, cedar trees, and carpets of bright green moss. Your cousin Lila is visiting and has joined you today for her first mountain hike.

Turn the page.

"Have you hiked this trail before?" Lila asks.

"Nope, but I've always wanted to," you reply. "There should be great views!"

You glance at your watch. It's almost noon. Normally, you wouldn't leave on a hike this late, but Lila slept in. The trail map on your phone says the hike should take five hours round trip. That should give you plenty of daylight. You grab your backpack, filled with food, water, extra clothes, matches, a pocketknife, and a whistle.

"Did you pack food and water?" you ask.

"I did—it's heavy!" Lila answers. You laugh.

Soon, you're surrounded by birdsong and forest. You march steadily, smiling as a pileated woodpecker swoops past. You glance back to show Lila, but she's not there.

Where is she? You wonder. You wait. Soon, she appears from around a bend.

"It's beautiful," she says. "But steep."

You nod in agreement, but you're a little worried. If she's tired already, will she be able to keep going for five hours?

"I forgot to tell my parents our hike plan," you say. "I'll text now." But your phone is not in your pocket. You rummage through your backpack. It's missing.

"I forgot my phone," you say.

"Just use mine," Lila says. "It's half-charged. I don't want to go back to the car."

"Um, okay," you say. But you feel uneasy. You tap out a text. Thankfully, your mom made you memorize her number.

Turn the page.

You carry on with your hike. Soon, Lila is breathing hard. You stop at a fork in the trail just as a trail runner descends from the left.

"Does that lead to the summit?" you ask him.

"It's a shortcut, but it's not on the map," the runner replies, and keeps going.

You peer up. It's steep and rocky, but so is the main trail. You only have so many hours of daylight, and Lila's pace is slowing you down. A shortcut might be good.

- To take the shortcut, go to page 15.
- To stick to the main trail, turn to page 24.

To make up some time, you choose the shortcut. You had high hopes, but as you climb up over gnarled roots and sharp granite, the trail deteriorates. You begin to second guess your decision. Your foot skids on loose rock, and you grab a root to steady yourself. You glance back to see Lila grasp a root and heave herself up a steep step. She pauses, breathing hard.

Turn the page.

The shortcut skirts close to the edge of a cliff. You tread carefully, gripping branches for balance. Then, at a mossy boulder, the trail disappears entirely.

"Which way?" Lila asks.

"Um, that way?" you guess, pointing past the boulder. You wish you knew for sure.

"Let's scramble over it," you say, gripping the edges of the boulder and hoisting yourself up.

"Whoa!" Lila screams.

You look back. Lila clutches a grizzled tree, her right leg dangling over the boulder.

"Give me your hand," you say.

You grab hold of a tree, grab Lila's wrist, and pull. She springs up, and you both slide down the other side of the boulder, breathing hard.

"That was a close call," you say. Now what?

"Do you want to keep going?" you ask Lila.

"I'm not sure," Lila answers, looking shaken from her near fall. "I did want to make the summit. Let's check the map." She takes out her phone. The battery is dead. You'll have to decide without a map.

"If we can find the shortcut again, I think we can head to the summit," you say. "Or, if we decide to go back down, we'll find a different way—not over that boulder again!"

- To keep going, turn to page 18.
- To look for another way down, turn to page 28.

"It might actually be safer to go to the summit and then find our way back down. There, we can find the marked descent trail back to the parking lot."

"Fine," Lila says.

"There," you point to a path free of moss. That's a sign that it has been walked on. "I think that's the shortcut. I bet we're almost at the summit."

You walk without talking. The trail is steep, and you are trying to save your energy. The views will be worth this difficult climb. Minutes drag by. An hour passes. Each step becomes more difficult.

"The trees are thinning," you say. "We might be close to the summit!"

With a surge of energy, you keep going. The ground beneath you has changed. It's no longer so steep, and instead of a path with small rocks and roots, it's more solid stone.

"Look!" you say. "I think we're there!"

You emerge onto a slab of granite dotted with windblown trees.

"Wait," you stop. "We should see the harbor. This isn't the summit."

"But then where are we?" Lila asks.

"I'm not sure," you admit. At some point, you must have veered off the shortcut. The sky glows pink and red. Soon, the sun will set.

"We need to decide if we'll keep going, or if we shelter for the night," you say.

Turn the page.

"Stay the night?" Lila's eyes widen. "That doesn't sound good."

"True, but we're not making the summit," you reply. "We need to either hurry down or stay put. It's going to get dark fast."

- To stop for the night, go to page 21.
- To hurry down, turn to page 30.

"We should make shelter," you say. "Walking around at night is dangerous."

"Check this out!" Lila says, pointing to large boulder with a natural overhang.

"Good start," you say. "The overhang will help keep us dry. Let's gather branches to lean against the boulder to build a wall."

You both grab branches and cedar fronds to create a wall and floor for your shelter—you are racing against daylight.

Just outside your shelter, you form a fire pit on soil with a ring of rocks, then pile moss, twigs, and branches. You will make your fire close but not too close to your shelter.

You hear a branch snap.

"Look!" Lila clutches your arm.

Turn the page.

A black bear stands about ten feet away. You freeze.

"Hi bear," you say calmly. You take Lila's hand and take a step back. The bear yawns and continues walking. You stay still and watch the bear walk out of sight.

"Whoa—that was close!" Lila says. "Should we build our shelter somewhere else?"

"There are bears everywhere," you say. "Let's stick here but get the fire going."

You start a fire and share your remaining food and water. There isn't much left.

"I'm still hungry," Lila says.

"I think those are huckleberries?" You point to a bush. "I'm pretty sure they're edible."

- To eat the berries, turn to page 33.
- To not eat the berries, turn to page 34.

You stay on the main trail, but it's taking Lila longer and longer to reach each trail marker.

"Let's hurry so we can see the view at the summit!" You say.

Lila hurries, her breath heavy, her face red and sweaty. Finally, you reach the top and are rewarded with amazing views. Huge boats bob in the harbor. The city glints with glass towers. Lila plops down on a granite slab.

"Wow. It's amazing, but I'm exhausted."

"That was a tough climb," you say. "Let's snack and start down." You have an energy bar and some water and start walking.

Branches brush your arm—the trail seems strangely narrow.

"Is this the same trail?" Lila asks.

Looking around, you don't see any trail markers.

"Um, I'm not sure," you say. You've already descended a long way, and Lila is so tired. "Let's keep going. We'll probably connect back with the main trail at some point."

The trail steepens, and you hear rushing water. You definitely don't remember that from the way up. Suddenly, the trail ends at a cliff. To your left, a waterfall tumbles over the edge. To your right, there is a ten-foot drop.

If you can make it down the cliff, a small ledge connects to the forest below. Descending those ten feet will be treacherous—but climbing back the way you came seems exhausting.

- To climb down, turn to page 26.
- To go back up, turn to page 35.

We only have to make it there," you point to the flat spot about ten feet down. "I'll go first."

You grip the top edge, fumbling until you find a footfall. Nervously, you slowly lower to another groove. You move down again, but your foot skids on moss, and you lose your grip.

"Whoa!" you yell, as you fall about five feet, knocking your head on the way down.

"Are you okay?" Lila yells from the top.

"I think so," you reply. You reach up and feel blood where you gashed your head.

You landed on the flat area that juts out to yet another cliff. To your left, the waterfall rushes down spraying mist. To your right, you see the path that, from above, looked like a safe way back into the forest. But from here, you see the ledge is narrower than you thought.

"Stay there," you say. "It's not safe for you to descend here."

"What about you?" Lila says. "That ledge looks narrow. Why don't you just stay there, and we'll wait for a rescue?"

This hike has gone terribly, and it's your fault. You have to do something. You feel unsure about crossing the narrow ledge, but it's short. Only a few steps and you'd be safely off the cliff.

- To walk the ledge, turn to page 37.
- To stay where you are, turn to page 39.

You're disappointed to turn back, but that was a close call.

"Let's think," you say. "Do you remember anything specific right before we got to the boulder? Big trees? Funny shaped rocks?"

Lila thinks for a moment. "When I looked up at one point, I noticed a blackened tree trunk, like it had been hit by lighting."

"Let's look for that," you say, excited. It feels good to have a plan.

You carefully pick your way through the forest, staying away from the cliff edge.

"That's it!" Lila points. Ahead, you spot the blackened tree and then the path.

"Yes!" you say. You follow the path, checking in with each other to make sure you are still on the same shortcut you went up. Finally, you reach the fork where you left the main trail. Watching the trail markers carefully, you return to your car.

"Well, we didn't make the summit, but it will make a good story," you say.

"True," Lila responds. "But next time, I'm not taking the unmarked shortcut. Now I'm hungry, let's go find some dinner!"

THE END

To follow another path, turn to page 9.
To learn more about mountain survival, turn to page 99.

"We better move fast," you say. "Let's walk downhill. Hopefully, we'll cross the main path."

The forest is darkening rapidly. You push through brush and study trees and rocks. Did you pass this one before? That one? You are feeling panicked. You need to reach safety before sundown. Every shadow and sound feels like a threat.

A branch snaps. You stop, and Lila bumps into you. Bushes rustle. You hear a snuffling sound.

"What's that noise?" Lila whispers.

Your heart pounds. Could it be a bear? If so, you should speak quietly and back away—black bears don't like to be surprised or cornered.

Before you can stop her, Lila runs.

"Wait, don't run!" you say.

But you're too late. A black bear emerges from behind a fallen log. You can smell its musky scent. You are close—too close. By running, Lila likely triggered the bear's chase response, and black bears are surprisingly fast.

The bear charges, mouth open, ears flattened. One paw swipes your arm, claws digging into your skin. You feel the heat of its breath. The bear charges one more time, then pads off into the forest.

"Put pressure on the wound," Lila says.

You try, but your arm won't stop bleeding. You feel woozy and sick to your stomach.

"Let's keep going," you say. "I don't want to see that bear again."

Turn the page.

Without a plan, you stumble through the darkening forest. You trip and fall into a stream, soaking your clothes and your bag. You shiver and your teeth chatter.

"Are you okay?" Lila asks, her voice panicked. "Where are we?"

Unfortunately, you don't know.

"We have to stay warm," you say. You and Lila curl up under a bush. You pull a few fallen cedar boughs over your legs for warmth. But it's not enough, and hypothermia sets in quickly when night falls. As you begin to lose consciousness, you hope that someone finds Lila. Unfortunately, you are one of many hikers who never made it back from an afternoon hike.

THE END

To follow another path, turn to page 9.
To learn more about mountain survival, turn to page 99.

You both stuff berries in your mouth.

"Ugh! So sour!" Lila says.

"Maybe they aren't ripe," you say, spitting them out.

Hours later, you start vomiting. Maybe they weren't huckleberries after all.

In the morning, you stumble up and realize you are mere feet from the main trail. Lucky for you, a group of hikers comes by. They let you know that a search party is on its way now. You won't feel well for a day or so, but you survived.

THE END

To follow another path, turn to page 9.

To learn more about mountain survival, turn to page 99.

"It's dangerous to eat wild food that you can't 100 percent identify," you say.

"Yeah," Lila says. "Being poisoned for a measly few berries isn't worth it!"

You try to chuckle. It's best to keep your spirits up. You both drift off to sleep and wake to sunshine.

"Um, take a look," Lila points.

An orange trail marker is about 10 feet from your shelter. You look at each other and laugh.

You start down. You pass a group of hikers who tell you that a search party is getting started at the trail head. You race down—your parents will be so glad to see you!

THE END

To follow another path, turn to page 9.
To learn more about mountain survival, turn to page 99.

"We have to go back up," you say.

Lila agrees. You head back up using exposed roots as handholds to help you ascend. Finally, the trail flattens, and you are back in denser forest. Just ahead, you see a tree filled with woodpecker holes. You remember seeing it on the way up.

Turn the page.

"Do you see that shine?" Lila points. "On that tree." You squint. Could it be?

"An orange trail marker!" You exclaim.

"Yes!" Lila squeals. You both scramble towards the marker, giddy with relief.

You and Lila carefully follow the orange trail markers down. You reach the car as the first star appears. You're so relieved. You know this hike could have turned out badly. You hop in the car, crank the music, and head home.

THE END

To follow another path, turn to page 9.
To learn more about mountain survival, turn to page 99.

The narrow ledge is made of jagged, uneven granite. But in only a few steps you'll be off the cliff and can get help for Lila. You feel terrible that she's alone above you.

You wipe a drop of blood from your eyes. You gashed your forehead badly and are a bit dizzy. You hope you don't have a concussion.

Heart pounding, you step onto the ledge. You take another step, placing your foot carefully. Another step. You feel the cold air from the gully beneath you.

You look down—bad idea. It drops at least a hundred feet. Your head starts to spin. Your heart is racing. You're panicking, and you know it, but you don't know how to stop.

Turn the page.

You take a large step, and your foot slips. You catch yourself but now are in a full panic. Your legs shake. Your eye tears up. You want off this ledge.

You take another large step, and your foot slips again, and then you are falling with nothing to hold onto. Your decision to cross a too-narrow ledge was terribly foolish. Your last thought is that you hope Lila survives.

THE END

To follow another path, turn to page 9.
To learn more about mountain survival, turn to page 99.

"The ledge is too dangerous to cross," you call up. "We're trapped. Try to stay warm. Let's bundle up. Sit on your bag or a pile of leaves."

You are hopeful of a rescue because you texted your mom your plan. You sit as far from the waterfall as you can. You must try to stay dry to reduce the chance of hypothermia. You pull your extra layer out of your bag and curl up tight, piling moss and leaves over you for insulation.

The next morning, you repeat three whistle blasts regularly—the universal distress signal. It pays off. By late morning, you are found by search and rescue, who had been alerted by your parents. You are hypothermic and have a concussion, but at least you're both alive.

THE END

To follow another path, turn to page 9.
To learn more about mountain survival, turn to page 99.

CHAPTER 3

CRATERS OF COSTA RICA

You clutch the truck's arm rest as it bounces along a rutted path. The rough ride will be worth it as soon as you arrive at the field station. You are here to study the mountain life of Costa Rica. You can't wait to see the lush jungle, river canyons, and volcanic craters! You peer out the window as the truck bumps over the ruts.

"How many poisonous snakes are there here?" Marcus asks. He is one of the four students in the truck with you, along with the driver.

Turn the page.

"There's the pit viper and the Fer-de-Lance," you answer.

The driver speeds up to clear a puddle. Water sprays everywhere and then—*THUD!*

With a jolt, the truck lurches to a stop. The driver leaps out and looks underneath the truck.

"Deep pothole," he shakes his head. "The undercarriage is damaged. We're going to have to call for another truck."

You groan. What a waste of time. You need to get to the field station. The other half of your group was in another truck ahead. Maybe they can send that truck back to pick you up. The driver radios the other truck. No response.

"We'll keep trying," he shrugs.

Frustrated, you climb out of the truck. Outside, you feel like you're inside a cloud. Costa Rica lies between the Pacific Ocean and the Caribbean Sea, and warm moist air creates perpetual clouds—but also the dense, lush jungle.

You crouch down to examine a line of ants. They are huge! Maybe you should grab your camera and capture the moment since there's nothing else to do but wait. Then, you think about the field station. It's equipped with viewing platforms in the trees! The photos there would be much better. You wonder if it's within walking distance.

"How far is it to walk to the field station?" You ask the driver.

"A few hours," he replies. "It's a steep walk."

Turn the page.

"I'd walk with you," Marcus says. You're glad someone has volunteered, though Marcus tends to like reading more than walking.

The driver shrugs. "I won't stop you, but you don't know the area. So if I was you, I'd wait."

"But is it hard to find?" You ask. "Can you give us directions?"

"Follow the road up, and take the first left turn," he replies. "It will look like a rough road. That'll take you straight there."

"What if a new truck arrives soon?" Marcus asks.

"True," you say. "But the directions are simple. And I don't want to miss the field station's viewing platform at dusk tonight to see the nocturnal animals."

- To continue on foot, go to page 45.
- To wait by the truck, turn to page 49.

You put on your backpacks and start walking. Marcus has a field guide in his hand.

"Do you ever put that away?" you ask.

"Why would I?" he replies. "I like learning."

Good point, you think, and pull out your camera. There's so much to photograph. Moss, lichen, and vines grow everywhere.

Between taking photos, you spend a lot of time looking down. Every step could be dangerous out here.

Marcus has fallen behind, his nose in his field guide. You wait until he catches up.

"Have you seen a left turn?" You ask.

He looks up from his field guide. "Nope."

Turn the page.

Your back aches—your pack is heavy. You have matches, extra clothes, a flashlight, two water bottles, a whistle, and a couple of sandwiches. You eat a sandwich as you walk. Finally, you see a path to the left.

"Is that it?" Marcus asks.

"The driver said take the first left that looks like a road, right?" you say.

"Does this look like a road to you?" Marcus asks.

"I'm not sure," you say. "The path upwards looks more like the main path. It's wider."

The left path angles down, and is quite narrow, but it might fit a truck?

- To take the left path, go to page 47.
- To continue upwards, turn to page 55.

"I wish we'd asked whether there was more than one left turn," you grumble.

You are sweating and thirsty. You sip at your water. Marcus lags farther and farther behind.

"Can you get your head out of that book and hurry up?" you ask, your frustration mounting.

You wade through thick mud and jump puddles. Soon, your feet are soaked.

"Maybe we missed a left turn earlier and this is the wrong one," Marcus pants as he catches up.

"Maybe," you say, also feeling uncertain. "But the driver said it would take a few hours to walk. We're probably almost there." You hope.

As you walk, Marcus falls behind again. Every rustle in the trees creeps you out—what's out there? You stop to wait. Again.

Turn the page.

"Where is he?" you wonder.

You hear rushing water. Curious, you walk around a bend in the trail and through dense trees. The sound of water gets louder and louder until you see a waterfall dropping into a clear pool.

But now, you're surrounded by dense jungle and don't see the path you were on. And where is Marcus? How long ago did you lose him? You glance at the sky—it's darkening quickly. Something screeches from deep in the trees. You suddenly feel very alone.

- To go back for Marcus, turn to page 58.
- To wait where you are, turn to page 60.

It's probably safer to stay by the truck. You grab your camera and a granola bar and let your classmates know you're going to look around.

The vines, the plants, the sounds, and smells—everything is amazing! You see a tiny trail to one side. You scramble down to peek and see the volcano across the valley. You snap photos and keep following the trail. In the trees, you spot movement. You freeze. A small monkey swings by. Then another one. It's a troop swinging from tree to tree! Without thinking, you step off the trail and follow the monkeys. You get some incredible photos and can't wait to tell your group.

Finally, you stop and find yourself surrounded by dense jungle. You were so busy chasing the monkeys you lost the trail. How far did you go? Nothing looks like the path.

Turn the page.

"Help!" you yell. "I'm over here!"

No one responds.

You need to find your way back. You don't have any supplies with you except your camera and a snack. But aren't you supposed to stay where you are if lost?

You check your watch. You've already been gone an hour! They must have missed you by now. It's eerie in the jungle all alone. You can either stay here and consider your options, or you can try to retrace your steps.

- To stay put, go to page 51.
- To try to retrace your steps, turn to page 62.

Don't panic. You repeat this to yourself, while you gather your thoughts. You need a plan. You stay quiet and listen in case someone is calling your name. You hear birds singing and insects buzzing but no voices.

But you do hear rushing water. You think it's coming from your left. Hoping for a better view, you walk a short ways and catch a glimpse through thick trees of the valley, where a river winds through.

Earlier, your group had crossed the river. You could find the bridge, and then you'd know where you are! But if you leave this area, you'll be farther away from potential rescuers.

Minutes drag as you stay and listen for signs of a search party. You hear nothing.

Turn the page.

You wait and wait, but you're worried. It will get dark soon. You might need to take matters into your own hands. You consider your options. You could go to the bridge by the river like you thought before. Or maybe you can leave yourself a trail of markers and try to find your way out.

- To hike to the river and find the bridge, go to page 53.
- To create your own chain of trail markers, turn to page 65.

You hike to the river. If you find the bridge, you can walk to the small hotel you stayed at last night. It wasn't far from the bridge, maybe a ten-minute drive. But which way should you go?

You remember the pictures you took on the ride to the bridge. They might help you now.

You compare the photos on your camera to what you see now. The cone-shaped peak to your left looks familiar. You head off in that direction along the riverbank.

You are hot and thirsty. It's tempting to drink river water, but you know that might make you sick. You put your camera down and splash water on your face, hoping it will trick your body into feeling refreshed. But as you lean forward, the earth gives way, and you slip into the river.

Turn the page.

Gasping, you climb out, your clothes dripping wet. Maybe looking for the bridge is a foolish idea. Wet clothes make it difficult to stay warm and increase the chance of hypothermia.

It might be wiser to dry your clothes and hunker down for the night. A search team is bound to be looking for you by morning.

- To keep searching for the bridge, turn to page 67.
- To dry your clothes, turn to page 69.

You continue upwards, but soon, the trail narrows. You wonder whether a truck would fit.

"This feels wrong," you say. "Maybe we missed an earlier left turn. Let's make a plan. If we don't reach the field station in half an hour, we turn back."

"Fine," Marcus says.

You continue, but soon, you are trudging through dense trees coated with twisting vines.

"Let's turn back," you say. Thankfully, Marcus agrees. "Ugh!" You whack an insect off your arm.

"How long do you think it will take to return to the truck?" Marcus asks. You slap another mosquito.

"I'm not sure," you say. "Things look different going the other direction. Soon, it will be dark, and you don't know how far you'll need to walk. Your heart sinks, as you realize your only option is to spend the night in the jungle.

"We're stuck for the night. Let's start a fire," Marcus says. "It might ward off wildlife like big cats and help with the bugs."

You find a clearing and use a stick to clear the area of brush—you don't want to sit on a snake! Marcus lights a fire with a lighter he brought. The two of you eat your remaining food.

"Let's take turns sleeping," you say.

"Good call," Marcus says. "One of us can watch for dangerous animals.

It's a long night. When the sun finally rises, you continue retracing your steps.

"Let's see if we missed a left turn," you say.

Finally, you see it: A left turn that heads upwards.

"How did we miss this yesterday?" you fume.

You hear the rumbling of a truck. It's your group! They've been looking for you.

"We were worried," the driver says. "We're glad to see you." On the bumpy ride to the field station, you tell your story of survival. Next time, you'll think twice about heading into unfamiliar territory.

THE END

To follow another path, turn to page 9.

To learn more about mountain survival, turn to page 99.

In a panic, you turn back. You can't stay here alone. You move hastily, tripping and stubbing your toe.

How far back could Marcus be? Did something happen to him?

Soon, it's dark. You remember reading that Costa Rica is near the equator, so twilight here is shorter than in North America.

Your mind spins with questions: *Am I on the same path I came up? Did Marcus take a different path? Is a jaguar watching me?*

Exhausted, you flop down in a mound of dried brown palm fronds. Something moves beside you. A snake darts out of the fronds, and its fangs sink into your flesh. It's a venomous Fer-de-Lance, the deadliest snake in Costa Rica.

You should have known not to sit without first checking the area for dangerous creatures. There is an antivenom, but you don't have it. Sadly, by the time they find you the next day, it's too late. You don't make it.

THE END

To follow another path, turn to page 9.
To learn more about mountain survival, turn to page 99.

You remind yourself not to panic. You wait and wait for Marcus. He never arrives, but darkness does, along with an eerie hum of insects. You click on your flashlight. You'll rest a few minutes then make shelter. You lean against a tree and close your eyes. But rest turns to a deep sleep.

Sometime later, a piercing howl jolts you awake. Something rustles nearby. Another howl fills the air. The rustles get closer. Your heart pounds. What is it?

You don't wait to find out. You leap up, grab your bag, and run. In your haste, you slip down a rocky incline and splash into water, hitting your head on a rock. Stunned, you manage to crawl out of the water. You are on a small flat spot next to a lake, and you see the faint light of dawn.

You know you panicked—you stop and take a deep breath and think. You need to try to signal potential rescuers. You pull your bright-orange raincoat from your bag, spread it on the ground, and lie down, your head throbbing.

Later, a search party finds you—they saw you from a viewpoint above. You have a concussion and are dehydrated. Marcus was also found. He had fallen and broken his leg. Sadly, you'll miss the field study in order to recover. But you'll think twice next time about wandering off in an unfamiliar area. Most importantly, you're glad to be alive!

THE END

To follow another path, turn to page 9.
To learn more about mountain survival, turn to page 99.

You need to get to safety quickly. You hurry back in the direction you think you came from. How could you have followed the monkeys off the trail? Those photos better be worth it. You feel more and more panicked. Then, you hear a sound. It's mechanical. Could it be the truck? You run towards the sound. It's getting louder.

"Help!" You yell.

A small propeller plane flies overhead. You stop. There's no way that a plane is already out looking for you. Dejected, you stop.

"Help!" You yell again.

To your right, the terrain rises steeply. If you went up, you might get a better view of where you are.

You check your watch. You've been gone for two hours. It's almost dinnertime, and near the equator, it gets dark soon after dinner.

The thought of being in the jungle at night gets you moving. You start climbing. Sharp rock pokes into your hand as you grip rocky edges and low tree branches. Vines slap your face.

You reach for another branch, but it breaks off. You tumble down the steep incline, smashing your leg before landing in a heap. You try to get up but can't—your leg might be broken.

Turn the page.

You scream for help. You use the flash on your camera to try to signal someone. The pain in your leg is intense, and you slip in and out of consciousness. You can only hope that a rescue team finds you before a wild animal does.

As you lie there, you regret panicking and wish you'd stopped to think. Instead, you ran in the opposite direction of where the search party had set out. Unfortunately, they don't find you in time.

THE END

To follow another path, turn to page 9.
To learn more about mountain survival, turn to page 99.

Using your teeth to rip your thin orange shirt, you tear strips off the ends of your sleeves. You tie them as markers and begin to walk in the direction you believe you came from. That way, you'll know you aren't walking in circles.

"Help!" You shout. "I'm over here!"

Soon, you've used up all your trail markers. You could keep walking, but you might end up turning in a circle.

You keep yelling. "I'm over here!"

"Stay there! We hear you!" someone says

You are so relieved to hear Marcus's voice! Soon, your group and a few people you don't recognize are there.

Turn the page.

"We were so worried!" Marcus says. "Thankfully, another truck came, and we all came to look for you."

You thank everyone. You're grateful, relieved, and a bit embarrassed. Next time, no chasing monkeys!

THE END

To follow another path, turn to page 9.
To learn more about mountain survival, turn to page 99.

You are determined to find the bridge. You trek on, but you're exhausted, and the riverbank is slippery. As dusk falls, your teeth chatter. So much for being in the warm tropics.

You slip and fall into the river again. You are so tired that all you can do is float along, clutching a log. Luckily, it's going in the direction you want to go.

Finally, you reach the bridge! You swim to the riverbank with all your might. You flop onto it, numb and shivering, and pass out.

When you wake up, you are on a stretcher being rushed to a hospital.

"Thank goodness we found you," Marcus says as he sits with you in the back of the ambulance. "The medics think you have hypothermia."

For several days, you stay in the hospital and fight for your life. Thankfully, you make it. But one foolish decision almost cost you your life.

THE END

To follow another path, turn to page 9.
To learn more about mountain survival, turn to page 99.

You wiggle out of your wet clothes and lay them in the sun. Dry clothes will be key to survival once night falls and it gets colder.

While you wait, you gather large fern and palm fronds and place them on an angle off a low boulder. Dusk falls, and you check the ground for critters before piling more fronds to sit on. You eat your emergency snack. Finally, your clothes are dry. Exhausted, you manage to fall asleep in your shelter.

In the morning, you are thirsty, hungry, and lost. No one knows where you are. It's important to make sure rescuers can find you. Your group must be looking for you. Without matches, you can't light a fire to signal for help. You'll have to think of something else.

Turn the page.

You build a huge HELP sign in the clearing using branches and fronds. You wait. Finally, you hear a helicopter! As the helicopter hovers above, two rescuers are lowered on ropes by a winch.

"Are you okay?" one asks.

"I'm okay," you answer. "But thirsty."

After a drink, you are raised into the helicopter. You'll have a good story, but first you'll have to recover from severe dehydration.

THE END

To follow another path, turn to page 9.

To learn more about mountain survival, turn to page 99.

CHAPTER 4

ADVENTURE IN THE ALPS

"Snowball fight?" Your little brother, Finn, asks with a grin.

"Later," you say. "Let's explore!"

Snowcapped peaks surround you. You feel on top of the world here in the French Alps. You arrived today with your parents and younger siblings, Jasmine and Finn, for a ski vacation. Pure mountain air, snow, and no school—could life get any better?

Turn the page.

"Let's check out the snowshoe trails," you suggest to Jasmine and Finn. "Maybe there's time for a snowball fight and snow angels too."

"Don't be long," Mom says. "The sun will set in an hour or so. And stay on marked trails."

"Got it," you say. "I've got my daypack." Inside it is your phone, snacks, water, a small first aid kit with matches and a pocketknife.

You walk towards the nearby snowshoe trail marked with blue triangles. Jagged peaks line the distant horizon. The trail splits off through fir trees. You turn right here and left there. Your boots sink into fresh snow.

Suddenly, something whomps you from behind. Snowball time! Amidst the fun and laughter, it begins to snow. You take pictures of your siblings in the falling snow.

But before long, snow is falling furiously, and wind gusts through the trees. You should get back to the hotel.

"Let's go!" you shout.

"Which way?" Finn asks.

You look around for the blue trail markers, but it's hard to see even a few feet ahead of you. It's a blizzard.

"Hold hands!" You yell, grabbing hold of your siblings. But which way? You aren't sure. You trudge forward. In your hurry, you trip, tumbling off the trail into waist-deep snow. You stumble a few steps, but it's tough going in the deep snow. You have to find a trail marker before dark. But maybe you should call your parents.

- To look for a trail marker, turn to page 76.
- To call your mom for help, turn to page 80.

Your mom doesn't know where you are, so she couldn't help. Best to look for a trail marker.

"Follow my footsteps," you yell over blustery wind. With each step, you strain to lift your leg. You squint through blinding snow, searching for the blue triangle marker.

"Jasmine, hold the back of my coat. Finn, hold Jasmine's," you say. "Don't let go!"

"Where are we?" Jasmine asks.

Nothing looks familiar. You're in steep, forested terrain. And there's not much daylight left. Through the snowy trees, about 20 feet uphill, you see something shiny that could be a blue triangle.

"Do you see that?" you point.

You want to find the trail and return to the hotel's nice toasty fire and your parents.

Should you go see if it's a marker? Even though it's only twenty feet, it's uphill in deep snow to the possible marker, and cold wind is whipping across your face. Maybe you should you stop and try to warm up? The weather may pass quickly, and then you'll have the energy to try looking for the lodge again.

- To climb to the possible trail marker, turn to page 78.
- To build a shelter and light a fire turn to page 85.

You climb uphill using a switchback pattern, which zigzags back and forth horizontally. It's easier than climbing straight up. Even so, walking in the deep snow is exhausting.

"Up there," you say. "We're getting close!"

You finally reach what you thought was a trail marker and find a discarded blue pop can. Garbage. You kick it in frustration. Now what?

The snow has eased slightly, and through the trees, you spot what looks like a more open space. Could it be a ski run? If so, you could follow it down and find a ski chalet or someplace with people—and a phone.

"Let's see what's over there," you point. "Stay together!" Jasmine and Finn follow. You hurry—it will be dark soon.

You trek through trees and find yourself on the edge of an open slope. You see a twinkle of light in the distance.

"I think that's a building!" you say.

"Let's go," Finn says.

"Wait," you say. "I'm not sure we should cross this slope."

An open slope is the type of terrain where avalanches happen. But crossing it would be the shortest route to the twinkling lights. Or you could stick to the edge and cross at a spot with more trees.

- To head across the open terrain, turn to page 88.
- To stick to the edge, turn to page 90.

Your fingers are clumsy from being cold, but you manage to make the call. You get a message that the call cannot be completed.

"Try again," Finn says.

You call again, but the same thing happens.

"Maybe we need to be higher to get a cell signal," you say.

Snow swirls, and wind whips across your face. You can't see more than a few feet in front of you. You take another step and suddenly, you all tumble down a snowy incline. When you stop falling, you call out for your siblings.

"Jasmine! Finn! Are you okay?"

Thankfully, they are nearby and uninjured but covered in snow. You look around. The incline where you fell isn't too steep, and you want to get back to where you were. It's about thirty feet up, you estimate.

"Let's walk back up," you say. It's hard work, and soon, you are all panting with exertion.

"I'm so thirsty," Finn says. He reaches to shove snow in his mouth.

Turn the page.

"Wait," you say. "It's dangerous to eat snow. It's too cold for your body." You pull your water bottle out. It's almost empty, and Finn takes the last gulp.

"We'll have to melt snow to drink," you say.

You have a ways to go uphill before you reach the plateau you fell from. It might be your best chance to find the trail. On the other hand, everyone is cold and tired. Perhaps it's wiser if you stop to warm up and melt snow.

- To find a spot to melt snow, go to page 83.
- To keep climbing, turn to page 92.

While it's tempting to eat snow, it increases the danger of hypothermia. You are so glad you are wearing your ski parka—and that gives you an idea.

"Let's figure out a shelter," you say. "And let's try to melt snow using body heat."

You stuff snow into your empty water bottle and place it under your ski parka, in your hoodie's front pouch. By the time you build a shelter, some of the snow will hopefully have melted from your body heat. Meanwhile, the sun has set, and only faint light remains.

"It's almost dark," Jasmine says. "How will we get back?"

"I don't think we can tonight," you say. "We need shelter."

Turn the page.

"Let's build a snow fort," Finn says.

"That sounds difficult," you say. "Let's consider our options."

"Look!" Jasmine points to a spot about twenty feet away where the mountain rises up more steeply. "I see rocks. Maybe there's a cave?"

"Let's check it out," you say. You take a step, and your leg sinks to your knee. "Whoa!" you say. "I think it's a tree well."

You lean down and clear some snow off the lowest branches of the tree. "Look down there."

You see a hollow space under the lowest branches of the tree. You could take shelter there. But a cave would also be good.

- To check out the possible cave, turn to page 94.
- To use the tree well, turn to page 96.

Jasmine and Finn shiver. If you get too cold, you will all become hypothermic—deadly in a cold place with no shelter. You open your emergency kit with matches and a pocketknife.

You choose a spot out of the wind and start digging a trench in a snowbank with a big stick. You cover the shelter with evergreen branches. You place layers of leaves inside for insulation—sitting on snow will chill you.

"Let's gather material to burn," you say. "Look near the bottom of trees, close to the trunk, for dead branches. They might be the driest wood we can find." You call. "And look for brown evergreen needles and birch bark to help start the fire." You need as much fuel as possible.

Turn the page.

You build the fire just outside your shelter. You spark a match, but it doesn't start a flame.

"Everyone, check your pockets," you say. You find some crumpled paper and a handful of lint. You light another match. A flame catches on the paper and lint, then slowly lights the needles and bark, then the branches. Success! You crawl into your shelter.

It feels like the longest night in history. When you're not huddled together, you keep feeding the fire and focus on positive thoughts. Your parents will be looking for you. You just have to stay alive.

In the morning, you hear the best sound. *Thwock! Thwock!* It's a helicopter! You jump up and wave. The helicopter circles away.

Soon after, a search and rescue team on skis arrives. The helicopter pilot saw your fire and shared your location with the ground team. Your parents are waiting at the chalet, and you are so happy to see them!

THE END

To follow another path, turn to page 9.
To learn more about mountain survival, turn to page 99.

"Let's cross quickly," you say.

The slope is about the length of a basketball court. After that, you'll be in the trees and on your way to the twinkling lights and a phone call to your parents.

All you hear is your breathing and the stomping of three sets of boots in the snow. You are in the middle of an open slope where it just snowed heavily. It's a dangerous place to be. You try to shake those thoughts away.

You're halfway there. Each step feels like it takes forever. Suddenly, you hear a strange sound, like a whoosh.

"Hurry," you say. The sound gets louder, like a grumble. You try to run.

A wall of snow hurtles down the slope like a freight train. It's an avalanche! You are in the middle of the open slope.

"Run back to the trees!" You scream.

But it's too late. The decision to cross an open slope cost you your life.

THE END

To follow another path, turn to page 9.
To learn more about mountain survival, turn to page 99.

You stay on the edge and head down towards the lights.

"Stay close to the trees," you say, keeping watch that Finn and Jasmine stay away from the open slope.

Suddenly, you hear a whoosh from above. It's an avalanche!

"Hold tight to a tree!" You shout.

You grip tight to a trunk with Finn—just in time. On the open slope, a wall of snow hurtles past. You hold on for your life.

Jasmine screams as snow hits her tree.

"Don't let go!" you yell. She manages to hold on. When the avalanche stops, Jasmine is still there, but crying. She was crushed against the tree and broke several ribs.

If you'd been on the open slope, you'd have been swept away and buried. You're relieved, but it was a frighteningly close call. Keeping in the trees, you trudge down towards the lit-up building.

Jasmine can barely walk and must lean on you. By the time you arrive at the building, a warming hut, you are all hypothermic and ready to collapse. Thankfully, there are a few skiers there who help you and call your parents. Jasmine's injuries mean your trip will be cut short, but you were lucky—you survived.

THE END

To follow another path, turn to page 9.
To learn more about mountain survival, turn to page 99.

Mom and Dad must be so worried—you have to find your way back. Your feet and hands are numb. Your face feels raw from the wind. But you keep going anyway.

The wind gusts, and a spray of snow tumbles from a tree, covering everyone. It's shockingly cold. Everywhere around you is deep snow, and you are barely making any forward progress.

"We need to get out of the wind," you say.

"Let's pile up snow and dig a hole like a cave," you say. You don't know what else to do, and you can't imagine walking anywhere else.

Building a snow trench is hard work. You all begin to sweat and pull down your hoods. Snow collects under your collar and starts to melt. Soon, you are all wet. Finally, you dig a trench in a snowbank that you can all fit in.

You manage to throw in a few piles of evergreen boughs for insulation, but you are too tired to muster the energy to start a fire.

You huddle together and shiver. Your body temperatures are dangerously low. Through the night, you nod in and out of consciousness, wishing that you'd stopped earlier to make a proper shelter and light a fire.

At some point, you think you hear a helicopter, or is it just a dream? None of you wake up in time to find out. Your parents never recover from the loss of their three children.

THE END

To follow another path, turn to page 9.
To learn more about mountain survival, turn to page 99.

A cave seems like the safest option. The three of you trudge over to where Jasmine had pointed.

"An entrance!" Jasmine exclaims.

You have to duck, but you'll all fit. You are glad there are no critters inside. You all squish in.

"Let's cover the entrance with thick branches for extra warmth," you say.

You do so and then hang an extra shirt to seal it. Finally, you feel safe! You settle in and nod off.

You awake a while later with a headache. Something feels wrong. The air feels stale and still. You feel dizzy. You push aside the entrance coverings and take a gulp of outside air.

You remember watching the news about a group of people trapped in a cave. They ran low on oxygen!

"Wake up!" You shake Jasmine and Finn.

You clear the entrance to let air into the cave. You'd been breathing in oxygen and releasing carbon dioxide. Without new air coming in, eventually, you could have been poisoned. Thankfully, you ventilated the cave in time.

In the morning, you leave your cave. You start to make a plan, when a search and rescue team shows up on skis!

"Your parents will be glad to see you!" a rescuer says. "Do you want to give them a call on my satellite phone?"

You happily make the call. It was a close call in the cave, but you survived!

THE END

To follow another path, turn to page 9.
To learn more about mountain survival, turn to page 99.

"Tree wells are dangerous if you fall in headfirst, and they are filled with snow. But this one is mostly hollow, with branches that can serve as the roof. Ready-made shelter—almost!"

You all gather leaves and fallen branches. You pile up leaves to sit on and place branches around to reinforce the natural roof.

You curl up inside like a pack of wolves. It's surprisingly warm compared to outside, but fresh air is still coming in. You have a fitful night's sleep with the hope that you'll find your way back tomorrow.

In the morning, the snowstorm has passed, leaving a bright blue sky.

"I'm going to look around," you say. "Stay here."

You walk five minutes in each direction then return to your shelter using your own footprints. You see nothing but trees.

You walk again, this time going a few minutes farther in each direction. Still nothing but trees and snow. You remind yourself not to give up and imagine seeing your parents. You try again.

Finally, through the trees, you see a chalet! You gather your siblings and start to trudge towards it. At the chalet, everyone is thrilled to see you—an alert had gone out that three children were missing. Your parents are notified. And when they arrive, you get the best hug ever!

THE END

To follow another path, turn to page 9.

To learn more about mountain survival, turn to page 99.

CHAPTER 5

MOUNTAIN SURVIVAL

No one plans to get lost, but it happens. Mountains vary in terrain, weather, and wildlife. Each presents different survival challenges. Before leaving on an adventure, always tell someone your plan. Choose activities that match your ability. Check weather forecasts, and pay attention to your surroundings. Stay with your group. Allow plenty of time to return before sunset, and change your plan to stay safe if needed.

Preparation is key to survival. You should always pack the essentials. This includes a light, a whistle, matches or a lighter, extra clothes, a pocketknife, and a small tarp. You also need water, food, a first aid kit, a map, and a fully charged cell phone. Be aware that your cell phone may not have service.

Even when you've prepared, you can still end up lost. Don't panic. When you panic, you don't make good decisions, and this can have deadly consequences. Before acting, try to think and plan. If no one knows you're missing, you may need to rescue yourself. Otherwise, the best course of action is to stay where you are and survive. Don't wander aimlessly—this can make it harder for rescuers to find you.

To survive, you must prioritize your needs. First, deal with life-threatening issues, such as bleeding. Then, fire and shelter are critical. Most people who don't survive die due to hypothermia, not from lack of food or water.

If you're able to build a fire, do it. Fire will keep you warm, ward off animals, and signal potential rescuers. Control your fire to reduce the risk of wildfire.

If you can't start a fire, do what you can to draw attention to rescuers. Lay out colored items or use what you have to make help signals.

Shelter will keep you warm and dry. A cave can provide shelter, but it may be occupied by animals, and it must have air flow to be safe. A lean-to is a good emergency shelter. Lean branches onto a fallen log or boulder. Keep it small to trap in heat.

In a snowy location, dig a trench in a snowbank or tree well. Build a roof with whatever you have. Hypothermia can occur in any location if you are immersed in water. If you get wet, prioritize getting dry.

Stay alert and be prepared to encounter wildlife. Knowing how to respond to predators could save your life. Most animals don't want to approach humans, but they will if they feel threatened.

For water, find a lake, stream, or river. Boil water before drinking to avoid germs. As a last resort, use natural cloth, like cotton, and sand to filter it. In a snowy environment, melt snow to drink. Do not eat snow without melting it first. Snow will lower your body temperature, burn calories, and contribute to hypothermia. Drink the water you have, and try to avoid sweating.

You can survive more than a week without food. But without food, you will be weaker. Learning to identify edible plants is an important survival skill. It's best to never eat anything that you can't 100 percent identify.

If you are caught in a blizzard, find a safe shelter, and wait out the storm. Avalanches are a huge danger when traversing a snowy mountain. Avoid potential avalanche terrain. Beware of slopes with large treeless areas. Avalanches often occur during or after a big snowstorm. If you are in the vicinity of an avalanche, try to move to the edge and grab anything solid to keep from being swept away. If you are caught in the avalanche, try to move on the surface using a swimming motion.

TRUE STORIES OF MOUNTAIN SURVIVAL

ESTHER WANG

In June 2023, Esther Wang, 16, was hiking through the Coast Mountains of British Columbia with a group. Esther got separated from the group. Alone in unfamiliar territory, she remained calm. That night, she drank from a river and slept on rocks. By morning, Esther heard whistles and saw spotlights from helicopters above. But she was not able to catch their attention, as the forest was so dense. By the second night, exhausted, she sheltered under a tree. The next morning, she looked at pictures she had taken and recognized a landmark from early in the hike. Now she had a direction to head! She followed a river and found a gravel path which led her to a parking lot. She survived being lost alone for 54 hours.

CAROLYN AND RACHEL LLOYD

In April 2016, Carolyn Lloyd and her daughter, Rachel, went hiking in New Zealand's Tararua Range. On their ascent, they followed orange trail markers. But on their descent, they got lost. Their phone had no service. They skidded down a cliff. They sat in a tree for the night. Over the next few days, they followed a river, rationing supplies, and trying to stay hopeful. At one point, Rachel fell into a river and hit her head. Later, Carolyn built giant HELP signs using ferns and rocks. After 95 hours, a helicopter saw the signs and rescued them.

MARK GAYOWSKI

In December 2019, Mark Gayowski went out-of-bounds skiing on Red Mountain, British Columbia. At some point, he veered off course and got lost. His phone had no service. He tried climbing back up the mountain. Disoriented, freezing, and exhausted, he stopped to shelter under a tree and sleep. The next morning, he saw three people on skis. He had told his mom where he was going, and she had called for a search party.

S.T.O.P. TO SURVIVE

The best way to remember what to do if you find yourself in an emergency situation is to S.T.O.P. Each letter stands for an instruction you can follow to help get yourself to safety.

S.T.O.P.: Stop, Think, Observe, Plan

Stop: Stay calm and take in the situation.

Think: What do you need to do to survive? What supplies do you have on hand that you could use?

Observe: Look around. Do you see familiar landmarks? Can you tell what direction you're pointed?

Plan: Make a plan of action and never give up.

OTHER PATHS TO EXPLORE

1. In today's world, we have technology at our fingertips, such as GPS and helicopters that fly in the dark. But what might happen when we rely too much on technology? What do you think the pros and cons are of technology in a wilderness setting?

2. Search and rescue organizations often consist of highly skilled volunteers. They put their own lives at risk to search for missing people. How much danger do you think they should expose themselves to in order to rescue someone?

3. Mountain ranges vary hugely across the world, from snow-covered peaks to tropical ones. What survival skills might be common no matter the terrain? What skills and strategies might be different?

GLOSSARY

avalanche (AV-uh-lanch)—occurs when a large amount of snow slides suddenly down a slope

concussion (kuhn-KUHSH-uhn)—a brain injury resulting from a fall or a hard blow that can lead to headache, dizziness, and confusion

dehydration (dee-hay-DREY-shuhn)—occurs when too much water is lost from the body to maintain healthy functions

hypothermia (hay-puh-THUR-mee-uh)—dangerously low body temperature

navigate (NAV-uh-gayt)—to find one's way on, over, or through something or someplace

nocturnal (nok-TUR-nuhl)—active during the night

predator (PRED-uh-tur)—an animal that hunts other animals for food

ration (RASH-uhn)—to limit supplies to make them last for a longer period of time

tree well (TREE WELL)—a hole around the base of an evergreen tree that forms when low branches stop snow from settling around the trunk

READ MORE

Doeden, Matt. *Can You Survive: Hair-Raising Mountain Encounters?* North Mankato, MN: Capstone Press, 2023.

Eaton, Maxwell III. *Survival Scout: Lost in the Mountains.* New York: Roaring Brook Press, 2023.

Stroud, Les. *Wild Outside: Around the World with Survivorman.* Berkeley, CA: Annick Press, 2021.

INTERNET SITES

Forest Service U.S. Department of Agriculture: If You Get Lost
fs.usda.gov/visit/know-before-you-go/if-you-get-lost

National Geographic Kids: Mountain Habitat
kids.nationalgeographic.com/nature/habitats/article/mountain

Outdoors: How To Create a Shelter When You're Lost in the Woods
outdoors.com/how-to-make-it-through-the-night-if-youre-lost-in-the-woods/

ABOUT THE AUTHOR

Megan Clendenan is a children's book author and freelance writer. She loves reading and writing books about adventure, history, and the environment. Her middle-grade non-fiction books include *Fresh Air, Clean Water* (2022), which won the 2023 Green Earth Book Award, and *Cities: How Humans Live Together* (2023). She lives near Vancouver, British Columbia, with her family and two fuzzy orange cats.